ART DECO
FASHIONS COLORING BOOK

MING-JU SUN

DOVER PUBLICATIONS, INC.
MINEOLA, NEW YORK

Introduced on a grand scale at the 1925 Paris International Exposition, the new Art Deco style expressed modernity and embraced the new technologies that were rapidly changing the world. In the realm of fashion, it was the new "chic," representing glamour, luxury, and a sleek style. An exciting display of elegance and cool sophistication, this collection captures the lavishly exotic designs that were popular with fashion illustrators of the day. Interestingly, the device of using exaggeratedly longer proportions in depicting the fashionable figure became the standard. The pages in this book are unbacked so that you may use any media for coloring and are perforated for easy removal.

Copyright

Copyright © 2014 by Ming-Ju Sun
All rights reserved.

Bibliographical Note

Art Deco Fashions Coloring Book is a new work,
first published by Dover Publications, Inc., in 2014.

International Standard Book Number

ISBN-13: 978-0-486-78456-4
ISBN-10: 0-486-78456-8

Manufactured in the United States by RR Donnelley
78456807   2015
www.doverpublications.com